TONY ROBINSON'S
WEIRD WORLD OF WONDERS
EGYPTIANS

Illustrated by Del Thorpe

MACMILLAN CHILDREN'S BOOKS

The real **Nits** is a rescue dog. She's about twelve years old and has a wonky back leg because someone was cruel to her when she was a puppy. She's absolutely brilliant, although she does go *grrrr* sometimes when you pick her up. This book is dedicated to her.

Jessica Cobb is a friend of mine who knows much more than I do. She found out loads of stuff for me about the Egyptians which I was then able to put in this book. Frankly I couldn't have written it without her. It's great when you've got friends who make you look good, isn't it?

First published 2012 by Macmillan Children's Books
a division of Macmillan Publishers Limited
20 New Wharf Road, London N1 9RR
Basingstoke and Oxford
Associated companies throughout the world
www.panmacmillan.com

ISBN 978-0-330-53387-4

Text copyright © Tony Robinson 2012
Illustrations copyright © Del Thorpe 2012

The right of Tony Robinson and Del Thorpe to be identified as the author and illustrator of this work has been asserted by them in accordance with the Copyright, Designs and Patents Act 1988.

1 3 5 7 9 8 6 4 2

A CIP catalogue record for this book is available from the British Library.

Typeset by Dan Newman/Perfect Bound Ltd
Printed and bound by CPI Group (UK) Ltd, Croydon CR0 4YY

TONY ROBINSON'S

WEIRD WORLD OF WONDERS

EGYPTIANS

Tony Robinson has written lots of books about history and ancient stuff, including *Tony Robinson's Kings and Queens* and *The Worst Children's Jobs in History*, which won the Best Book with Facts category of the Blue Peter Book Awards 2007. He has also written several television series for children, including *Maid Marian and Her Merry Men*, for which he received a BAFTA and a Royal Television Society Award. He presents Channel 4's archaeology series *Time Team* and played Baldrick in *Blackadder*.

Del Thorpe has been drawing ever since that time he ruined his mum's best tablecloth with wax crayons. Most of his formative work can be found in the margins of his old school exercise books. His maths teacher described these misunderstood works as 'wasting time'. When he left normal school, Del went to art school and drew serious, grown-up things. Soon he decided the grown-up stuff was mostly boring, so went back to drawing silly cartoons and

C555104757

Other books by Tony Robinson

The Worst Children's Jobs in History

Bad Kids

Tony Robinson's Weird World of Wonders: Romans

Tony Robinson's Weird World of Wonders: British

Tony Robinson's Weird World of Wonders: Greeks

Hi! We're the Curiosity Crew. You may spot us hanging about in this book, checking stuff out.

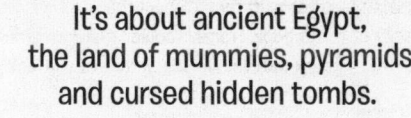

Grrr

It's about ancient Egypt, the land of mummies, pyramids and cursed hidden tombs.

It was also a country jam-packed full of extremely weird wonders. In fact there were more in Egypt than in any other country in the world.

Read on to find out . . .

Stig Grace Peewee Jojo

Nits

THE SEVENTH WONDER

There were **Seven** Wonders in the Ancient World...

The Statue of Zeus
at Olympia

The Lighthouse
of Alexandria

The Temple of Artemis

The Hanging Gardens of Babylon

The Colossus of Rhodes

The Great Tomb at Halicarnassus

All these six Wonders were destroyed long ago. But the **seventh** is still standing. It is . . .

The Great Pyramid of Egypt!!!

When it was built around four and a half thousand years ago, the Great Pyramid was the biggest building on Earth. In those days the tallest thing most people had ever seen was a really big tree. Can you imagine what they thought when they saw it?

It was over 140 metres high, and its base spreads out over an area of 13 acres (that's more than 8 football pitches).

But the Great Pyramid wasn't a one-off. Over a **hundred** pyramids are still dotted among the sands of Egypt.

So why were they built?

PYRAMIDIOTS!

The pyramids were built by the Pharaohs (pronounced FAIR-RO'S) – the rulers of Egypt. They were designed to keep the Pharaoh's body and soul safe after his death. The Egyptians believed that if they didn't watch over their dead Pharaohs, their gods would get angry and would punish them with drought, plague, invasion and an all-round rotten time.

So each pyramid was a giant tomb, and somewhere inside it was the coffin of the Pharaoh and the belongings he needed in the next life.

Now you're probably saying to yourself, '*I can see why they might decide to build a tomb to keep their dead ruler safe, but why did it have to be in the shape of a gigantic pyramid?*'

Well the answer to that is . . . errr!

Actually, I haven't a clue.

It's a question that even the experts can't answer. Rather annoyingly, the Egyptians didn't write down why they built pyramids . . . the pyramidiots!

POSSIBLE REASONS FOR BUILDING A PYRAMID

Maybe it was:

a) Because a pyramid looked like the first mound of earth that rose out of the sea when the world was created.

or

b) Because the Egyptians worshipped the sun, and a pyramid looked like the sun's rays (if you think of the sun shining through the clouds after a spot of rain, the rays are vaguely pyramid-shaped).

or

c) Because they thought the shape of the pyramid would help guide the Pharaoh's soul up into the sky where he could be united with the gods.

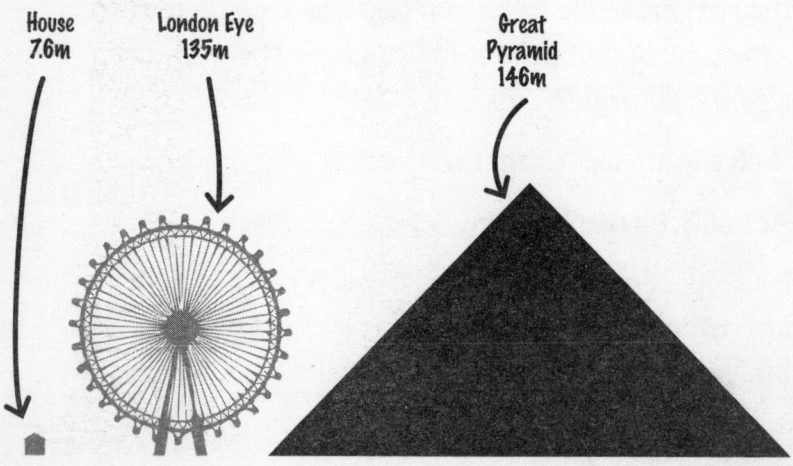

House
7.6m

London Eye
135m

Great
Pyramid
146m

or

d) Because they really liked Toblerone.

In fact it could have been any or all of the above, although my money is on **d)**.

One thing's for certain – the pyramids deliberately stood out, towering over everything else for miles around.

By building them, the Egyptian Pharaohs were showing how powerful they were.

It was their way of saying *'Check out how much cash I've got. I can put up the biggest building in the world. Aren't I brilliant? You can't do it, you dummy. Ha ha!'*

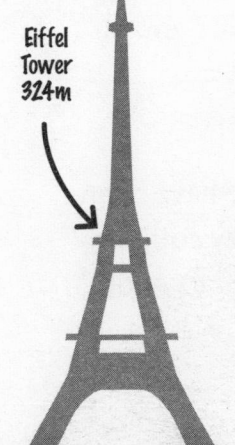

Eiffel
Tower
324m

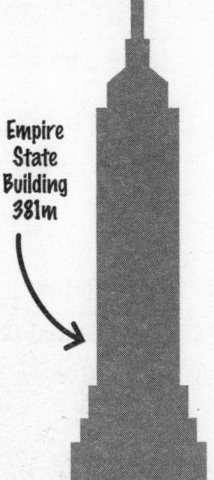

Empire
State
Building
381m

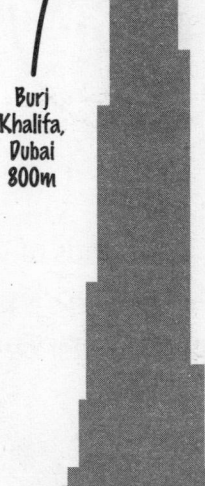

Burj
Khalifa,
Dubai
800m

WHO INVENTED PYRAMIDS?

Thousands of years ago when the people of our planet were ignorant and stupid, alien fish-men flew their spaceships down to Earth, landed in Egypt, built a pyramid, then flew off again.

Actually, that's rubbish!

Once upon a time a terrible flood engulfed the great city of Atlantis. The handsome giants who lived there escaped to Egypt, erected a pyramid like their ones back home in Atlantis, then disappeared.

That's double rubbish.

For thousands of years, though, people have been making up stories like this, because they couldn't believe ordinary human beings were smart enough to build them.

BUT HERE IS THE TRUTH

The ancient Egyptians built them all by themselves – and remember they didn't have cranes or cement-mixers or power drills like modern builders: they had to do it all by hand!

It took them a long time to learn how to make a proper pyramid, though. Their first attempts were frankly a bit lame. They were made out of mud bricks and were big and rectangular, like giant doorsteps. (In fact they were called **mastabas**, which comes from the Arabic word meaning 'bench', because that's what people who'd never seen a doorstep thought they looked like.) They certainly weren't very dramatic or stylish.

I suppose you've got to start somewhere!

That's a step in the right direction.

But then one day, an architect called Imhotep decided to try something a bit different. He built a mastaba out of stone, then he built another smaller one on top of it, then another even smaller one on top of that one, and he kept going until he'd built six mastabas one on top of the other – a bit like Lego (if Lego blocks were made of limestone instead of plastic, were over a metre high, and didn't have those knobbly bits on them).

What he'd created was the first pyramid. It's called a **step pyramid** for obvious reasons.

Step pyramids became all the rage – every Pharaoh wanted one, and they all wanted theirs to be bigger and better than the last one.

Then along came a Pharaoh called Snefru (quite a lot of Pharaohs had weird-sounding names: you just have to accept that they sounded ordinary to Egyptians). He decided he wanted to have something even more flash, a pyramid that was smooth rather than one with stepped sides.

This was obviously much trickier than plonking stone blocks on top of each other, and no one really knew how to do it. They started by building quite a steep sided pyramid, but then halfway through they had to change the angle to prevent it collapsing. So what they ended up with was a very wonky pyramid. Miraculously, it's still there today. It's actually known as the **Bent Pyramid**!

Almost there!

But Snefru wasn't happy with his Bent Pyramid – and you can't blame him. He told the builders to go away and think of something else, and being the Pharaoh, they didn't argue with him.

So they built another one, known as the **Red Pyramid** because of the reddish stone used to make it. This time they got the angle right and the Red Pyramid was the first true pyramid! Phew!

A VERY ANCIENT EGYPTIAN GAG

Pharaoh Snefru is said to have been the subject of one the oldest recorded jokes.

Question: 'How do you put a smile on the face of a bored Pharaoh?'

Answer: 'Sail a boatload of young women dressed in nothing but fishing nets down the Nile and tell him to go and catch a fish.'

Maybe it's funnier in Egyptian?

To be honest, it isn't!

When he died, Snefru was buried in his Red Pyramid, and his son Khufu became Pharaoh. And guess what . . . Khufu immediately started work on his own pyramid. It was a great time to be pyramid builder – you were never out of work!

Khufu's was the fanciest pyramid ever constructed – the **Great Pyramid**. It was built using 2.3 million blocks of stone and although today it's a muddy brown colour, originally it would have been covered in polished white limestone and capped in gold. This would have reflected the sunlight and made it shine for miles around – it probably made the locals wish sunglasses had been invented.

JOJO'S HANDY HINTS FOR BUILDING A GREAT PYRAMID

1 First, dig up millions of lumps of rock.

2 Then take a copper chisel, chip a hole in each lump, stick a wooden wedge in them and whack them with a hammer to split them so they've got flat sides.

3 Repeat this until they're all rectangular.

4 Next load up all the split stone into a boat, and sail it up the Nile to the building site.

5 Now drag each block up a series of earth ramps to its place in the pyramid, using sledges, ropes and levers.

Finished!

6 Repeat every day for twenty years in the sweltering desert sun.

FRIDGAMIDS

The stone blocks used to build the Great Pyramid weigh on average **2.5 tons**.

Other things that weigh 2.5 tons:

Have we forgotten anyone?

A pick-up truck

22 refrigerators

A humpback whale

Because building pyramids was such a tough job, people used to think that the Egyptians used slaves to do it. Surely free men wouldn't want to? Why would they choose to do all that heavy lifting unless they had somebody with a big whip standing behind them?

But now experts think that they were built by thousands of ordinary Eygptians helped by teams of professional architects and builders. Each year, when the Nile flooded, farmers had a few months when they couldn't farm the land. So instead of paying taxes they came to help build the pyramids.

Near the pyramids, archaeologists have found the remains of villages where the builders and their families lived. They certainly aren't slave quarters – the food on offer was too good for that. There were butcher's shops to supply meat, brewer's yards to make beer, even a massive bakery which could produce thousands of loaves of bread each week. So if you liked a pint of beer and a bacon sandwich, Egypt was the place for you!

And if you accidentally fell off a pyramid, or got crushed by one of the big blocks, there was even a doctor on hand ... Lucky you.

I WOZ 'ERE

There's graffiti scratched on the walls of some of the pyramids. It seems to have been written by ancient Egyptian builders, because it says things like

Khufu's posse

Pharaoh's drunken crew

(Actually that's my translation!)

Building the pyramids brought the people of Egypt together. Everyone – from stone pusher to priest – would have known they were helping to add to the glory of Egypt and ensure the survival of the Pharaoh into the afterlife.

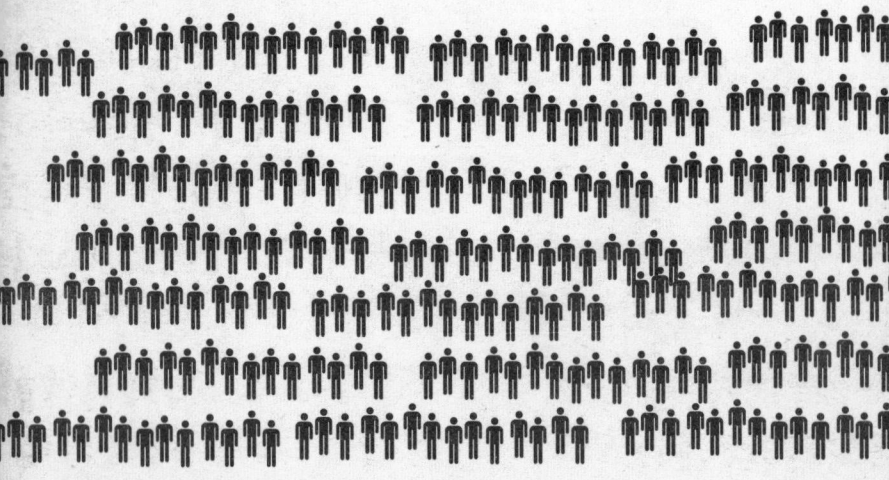

Grrrr!
We built this thing together, oooh! We're tough and rather clever, oooh!

THE SPHINX

Pyramids weren't built all on their own in the sand, miles from anywhere. Each one was at the centre of a whole complex of buildings including temples, other tombs for the Pharaoh's buddies, houses for the priests and workers, and some pretty amazing statues.

One of he largest statues in the world guards the pyramids at Giza, outside Cairo. It's a Sphinx, which was a monster with a lion's body and a human face.

It's a bit of a mystery – nobody knows who built it, when and why. No one wrote their name on it but it was probably put up around 2500 BC by one of the Pharaohs who built the pyramids. Most people think it was Khufu's son Khafre because it lines up with his pyramid, but others think it looks like his brother Djedefre.

Grrrr!

Experts believe it would originally have been brightly painted, but today the paint has worn off and the Sphinx has famously lost its nose and beard. That's what happens when you stand in the desert for three thousand years.

TOMB RAIDERS

At the heart of each pyramid was the Pharaoh's burial chamber: a stone room with a coffin containing his body.

Pharaohs were buried with everything they needed for the afterlife, and being Pharaohs what they thought they needed was lots of gold. Their coffins, stone cases called sarcophagi, were surrounded by gold furniture, gold statues, gold crowns, gold boxes full of gold – you get the picture!

So a pyramid was a bit like a giant neon sign with an arrow on it saying 'Gold this way!'

To stop robbers nicking all the gold stuff, some burial chambers were plugged up with stone after the Pharaoh had been buried. But robbers simply tunnelled through the stone and took the loot anyway! So later pyramids were built with twisty, turny tunnels, false corridors, secret staircases, trap-doors and dead-ends.

Unfortunately though, no matter how clever the pyramid designers were, robbers eventually managed to break into them. Not one pyramid has ever been found with its treasures intact!

Eventually Pharaohs stopped building pyramids and started digging hidden tombs in the hills instead. You can't really blame them, can you?

GUESS WHO'S AT THE BOTTOM OF THE PYRAMID!

Egyptian society was a bit like a pyramid – at the top, of course, was the **Pharaoh**. Being Pharaoh was a big job – he was the head of the government, the commander of the army and the chief priest of all the gods! Pharaohs were so special that you weren't allowed to touch them – even if you accidently touched a Pharaoh's crown you'd be put to death!

Then there was the **vizier**, who was a bit like the prime minister. He was the Pharaoh's most trusted adviser and the person who made sure all his orders were carried out.

Then a bit further down there were the high **priests** of the big temples, the military **generals** and chief **architects** – important men who had been given their post by the Pharaoh (often because they were related to him).

Next there were the **priests**, **doctors**, **lawyers** and **engineers** who had been lucky or rich enough to go to school.

Then there were all the **scribes** who wrote everything down. Writing stuff down was really important to ancient Egyptians but not everyone could do it – only the scribes. The reason we know so much about ancient Egypt is thanks to them!

Then there were all the **craftsmen** – the stonemasons, the artists, the carpenters and the metal-workers who made all the beautiful things Egypt was known for.

And finally way down the bottom was **you**! Well, not just you – all of us who farmed the land, carried the heavy stones and did all the rubbish jobs.

A LION IN THE FRONT ROOM

Egyptians didn't spend **all** their time building temples and pyramids. The grown-ups had work to do and families to look after, and the kids were just like you – they played games, messed about and got into trouble.

But the lives of the ancient Egyptians were pretty different to yours – for a start they lived in houses made of mud.

MESSING WITH MUD

In Egypt only buildings that were meant to last forever – like pyramids – were made of stone. Everything else was built of squidgy mud dug from the banks of the Nile.

There are two big advantages to building with mud – firstly it's free, and secondly there's lots of it.

How to make mud bricks:

1. Find a mould – the Egyptians used wooden moulds, but anything brick-shaped will do.

2. Dig up some nice wet, sticky mud, remove any stones and add straw to help bind it.

3. Push the mud into the mould – force it in deep so all the air and water is pushed out.

4. Tip the mould upside down so the brick drops out, and leave it in the desert sun to dry for several weeks.

5. Repeat 10,000 times and you'll have enough mud bricks to build a house. You'll also be very muddy.

I think we forgot the bit about letting the bricks dry.

The sun was good for drying mud bricks but it made life very hot and sweaty – so they tried to make their homes as cool as possible.

The houses of ordinary Egyptians had very small windows to keep the sun out, and were painted white to help reflect the heat. Most had flat roofs where they spent almost all their time – even sleeping there on hot nights. (Don't try this at home or you'll roll down the roof and into the street.)

Because there wasn't much wood in Egypt, their houses didn't have a lot of furniture in them (mud might be great for building houses but just try carving a chair out of mud or making a mud chest-of-drawers). Some homes only had a small table, a stool and a chest. But as Egyptians tended to hang out on the roof, this probably didn't bother them much.

Finally! Where have you lot been?

And just in case you were wondering, they didn't have bathrooms. If you wanted a shower, you went outside and tipped a bucket of water over your head. If you wanted to go to the toilet, there was a pot of sand, which you had to get rid of outside when it smelt a bit gross.

NUDE TEACHERS

If you turned up at school tomorrow without any clothes on you'd probably create a small riot. But ancient Egypt was so hot that often kids went around naked.

Even men and women usually wore nothing but short skirts (imagine your teacher dressed like that . . . No, probably best not to). They also rubbed their skin with perfumed oil to protect it from the sun and to help keep bugs away – just like we wear sun-cream or insect repellent on holiday.

Girls wore their hair in braids, or in pigtails hung with little weights to keep them straight, while boys shaved their heads except for a braided lock which dangled down one side of their face.

For special occasions, some men and women wore wigs and hair extensions. Sometimes these were made of vegetable fibres or sheep's wool, but if you were really posh you'd have one made of actual human hair!

Wearing a wig was a good way to stay cool – whenever it got too hot, you just took your hair off!

SQUASHING THE ENEMY

Most people went barefoot, but some had sandals with pictures of their enemy on the soles – so that whenever they wore them they'd be stamping on their foes!

While they weren't big on clothes, most Egyptians, even big hairy men and little kids, wore jewellery and make-up – not because they wanted to dress up as women, but because they believed it protected them from harm.

Before

After

They painted bright green or black lines around their eyes, using make-up made from ground-up minerals mixed with oil. They believed this would stop their eyes from becoming infected and would reduce the glare of the sun.

And they hung lucky charms called 'amulets' round their necks, ankles or wrists – amulets were precious stones carved in the shape of animals or insects, which they thought would keep away evil spirits.

SAND IN YOUR SANDWICHES

Egyptian children didn't rot their teeth by eating chocolate bars or drinking fizzy drinks – sugar wasn't discovered till centuries later. But there was something in the Egyptian diet that was bad for your teeth . . .

You know what it's like when you try and eat sandwiches on the beach, and a gust of wind blows little sprinkles of sand all over your cheese and ham roll. Well, it may not surprise you to know that because they lived in the desert, ancient Egyptians accidentally ended up eating lots of sand!

How do we know? Because experts have examined the teeth of dead Egyptians and have discovered they were worn down by a lifetime of chewing bread containing sand and grit!

Cairo from space, next to the Nile and an awful lot of sand.

DOGS, CATS AND DANCING MONKEYS

Ancient Egyptians loved animals and kept lots of pets.

Cats were very popular – they were believed to have magic powers and of course they were good at catching snakes and rats which was an added bonus. In fact cats were treasured so much that if you killed one you'd be put to death!

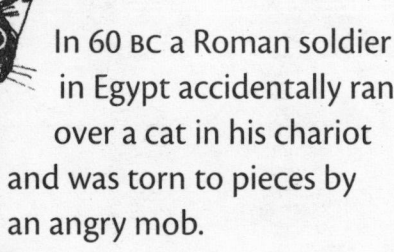

In 60 BC a Roman soldier in Egypt accidentally ran over a cat in his chariot and was torn to pieces by an angry mob.

Grrrr!

HOW TO WIN A BATTLE USING A LOAD OF CATS

In 525 BC, Persia attacked the Egyptian city of Pelusium. The Persian king knew how soppy the Egyptians were about cats, so he devised a plan: he ordered his soldiers to collect up loads of them, and just before the Persians charged, he released the moggies in front of his attacking army. Rather than run the risk of hurting the cats, the Egyptians immediately surrendered!

By the left, quick – miaow!

Dogs were so well-loved they were often buried with their masters. They had names just like we give our dogs names today (mine's called Nits). 'Brave One' was a popular Egyptian name; so were 'Good Herdsman' and 'Blacky' – there was even an Egyptian dog called 'Useless'!

They also had more unusual pets. Imagine having one of these in your house . . .

- **A Gazelle** – gazelles are a kind of antelope. The Egyptians kept them in their homes because they looked so cute.

- **A Dancing Monkey** – monkeys and baboons were really popular. Their owners sometimes dressed them up in clothes and jewellery, and there are even pictures of them dancing and playing musical instruments. Did they really do that, or was this just a fantasy? . . . I don't know!

- **Lions** – the royal families of Egypt kept lions. Scary? – Well, they probably had their claws and fangs removed before being turned into pets. So . . . scary, cruel and a bit ridiculous – I mean you'd have needed a pretty big litter tray, wouldn't you?

THE GAME CROCODILES LIKED

As for games, there was no satellite TV or Nintendo Wii around in those days, so ancient Egyptian kids had to make their own fun.

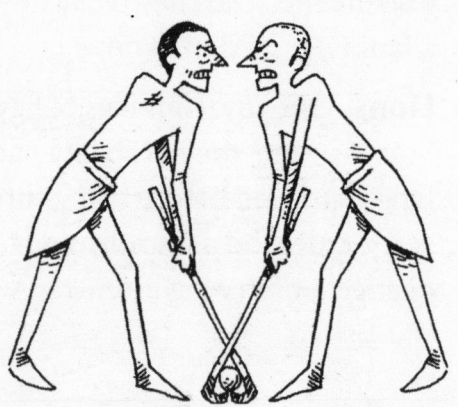

They played a game a bit like hockey using palm tree branches as sticks and a puck made from leather stuffed with reedy paper. There are also ancient pictures of kids wrestling, swimming and playing ball games.

There were water sports on the River Nile – one painting shows two teams of men in boats with long poles trying to push each other into the water. (The crocodiles probably thought this was a particularly good game!)

Board games were also popular, but unfortunately none have been found with the instructions, so it's pretty tricky working out how to play them. But one, known as 'Dogs and Jackals', may have been a bit like modern 'Snakes and Ladders'. The pieces either had dog's heads or jackal's heads and were placed in holes in the board. Coins were thrown to see how many moves each player could take. The first one to the end was the winner.

Toys were made out of whatever was cheap and easy to find – little children had rattles and model animals made out of clay. If your parents were rich, you might get a carved wooden toy like a hippopotamus with jaws that opened and shut, or a doll made of cloth and stuffed with reeds.

Animals bones also came in handy – instead of dice, Egyptians sometimes threw knucklebones – little squarish bones from the feet of sheep or goats!

Fancy a game of knucklebones?

I'll just put my hippo away first

LASSOING A PELICAN

Pictures show Egyptians hunting for lots of different types of birds, animals and fish that lived around the Nile. They used cats to flush ducks, geese, herons and pelicans from the marshes, and lassos, weighted ropes, bows and arrows and throwing sticks to bring them down when they were in flight.

A grilled pelican wrap. Yum!

BIG JOBS FOR LITTLE KIDS

With so many activities to choose from, you'd think being an ancient Egyptian kid would have been a lot of fun. You'd be wrong. It was hard work.

Ancient Egyptians loved kids and wanted as many as possible – but this was mainly so they could do jobs around the place!

From the age of five, children were expected to . . .

fetch food

sow seeds

bake bread

and **look after** their younger brothers and sisters.

At least they didn't have to load the dishwasher.

If they were from a wealthy family, boys might be sent to school to learn to be a scribe, while girls would be taught at home or be sent to serve in the temples as musicians or dancers.

Amenhotep was the scribe and architect of King Amenhotep III. What's that tucked into his belt?

SENSATIONAL SCRIBES

Scribes were the people who recorded events, wrote legal documents and kept the accounts.

At scribe school, boys learned reading, writing and mathematics. You had to practise your handwriting by dipping a reed brush in ink and writing on pieces of broken pottery (the ancient Egyptian equivalent of scraps of paper). If you messed around, the teacher would give you extra lines to write . . . and if you didn't do them he'd whack you with a rod until you did.

Teachers thought beating was an important teaching method – in fact the ancient Egyptian word for 'to teach' ('seba') also means 'to beat'!

SERIOUS WEIRDNESS

If you didn't much like being a kid, that was OK because you didn't have to wait long to be an adult. At thirteen you were thought to be grown up and your parents would start arranging for you to get married!

The Pharaohs of ancient Egypt had some particularly strange ideas about marriage . . . Most ordinary Egyptians thought that one wife or husband was enough, but Pharaohs often had several. One Pharaoh, Ramses the Great, had eight main wives as well as lots of minor wives and over a hundred children! Imagine the rows that must have gone on!

What's more, some Pharaohs didn't want to marry anyone outside the royal family – so they married their brothers and sisters instead! Which is just weird.

THE BEARDED LADY

Lots of ancient cultures didn't allow women to have jobs, or own land or help run the country. These were thought to be things that only men could do. Women had to stay at home, look after the family and do whatever their husbands told them.

But in ancient Egypt, things were very different. A woman could be a landowner, run a business or have a job in a temple or at court. And if she didn't like her husband, she could divorce him and choose another one.

Does my chin look big in this?

Women could even become Pharaohs – one of the most successful female Pharaohs was called Hatshepsut, and she ruled Egypt for fifteen years. But some people must still have had issues about women being rulers, because in order to encourage people to treat her like a man, she dressed in kingly clothes and even wore a fake beard!

HIPPOS AND FRIED EGGS

It might seem strange that one of history's greatest Empires was built in a desert – and not just any old desert . . . the **Sahara Desert** is one of the largest, hottest and driest places on earth. Temperatures can reach up to 68°C – that's so hot you could fry an egg on the ground, and a sausage and some tomatoes if you fancied it (although they might get a bit sandy)!

But it's not the heat that's the real killer in the desert, it's the **dryness**. Without rain nothing can grow: no trees, no plants, no earth.

Not a place you'd choose to live – unless you were completely insane.

But most ancient Egyptians weren't insane. They didn't live in the desert, they lived on the land around the River Nile, the river that flows northward through the Sahara to the Mediterranean Sea.

The Nile was the lifeblood of ancient Egypt – each year it flooded and covered the nearby ground with a thick black mud called 'silt'. Mud like this is great for growing things, and the land around the river was fertile and green.

The Nile was a very big deal to the Egyptians. It was their farm, their supermarket, their builder's yard and their playground. It allowed them to grow grain to make bread and beer, they used spears and nets to catch the fish and birds that lived in and around it, it provided water for drinking and bathing, the mud it deposited was used to make bricks for building, and the plants that grew on its banks were used to make boats, paper and even linen for clothes.

But it also had its dangers. Anyone who worked on the river or wanted to go for a quick swim had to be on the lookout for crocodiles and hippos. The word 'hippopotamus' comes from the Greek for 'water horse', although they don't look much like horses to me. I bet if you tried to ride one, it'd eat you. You don't get that with horses.

GODS WITH BEAKS

Imagine you've just shaved all the hair off your head; every single bit from the nape of your neck to your forehead. And you've shaved off your eyebrows, plucked out your eyelashes, and scrubbed your entire body in ice-cold water.

Now put on your clean white robe and your sandals made of reeds, and go outside. It's early morning and you're a bit shivery. There's no one else about. Ahead of you is a massive wall. Walk round it till you come to two vast stone towers decorated with images of the Pharaoh and the gods.

Go through the entrance between the towers. Now cross a big, open, paved courtyard with columns all around it and a big stone altar in the middle. Walk down a vast, gloomy, column-lined hall. At the end is a little door. Pick up an oil lamp from the marble table, and push open the door. Step inside. It closes behind you with a creak. You're in darkness – nothing but black silence. You hold up your tiny lamp.

Wait a minute. What's that in the middle of the room? Is it a creature? It's huge! You can see the glimmer of an eye; another eye; could that be a gold beak? And what on earth . . .

I've got a bad feeling about this . . .

You have just experienced the life of a young Egyptian temple priest. (Actually, the monster was just the statue of a god, but the priest would have thought it was real.)

The Egyptians had hundreds of gods, not just one big one like a lot of people believe in today. They had a god of war, a god of medicine, a god of animals, a god of weaving, and a god of sneezing. Actually, I'm not really sure about that last one, but it could be true, because you had to pray to the right god if you wanted to do virtually anything.

Think of all the things you do in a day.

If you were an Egyptian, as soon as you woke up you'd have to say a quick prayer to the god who made the sun rise.

On the way to school you'd pray to the goddess who protected children so you wouldn't get eaten by a crocodile.

When you took a school test you'd pray to the god of learning that you'd pass.

During lunch you'd say thank you to the god of the harvest.

On the way home you'd remind the god of your house to check that it was still standing.

And when you went to bed you'd have another word with the solar god to make sure that the sun would rise again the next day.

And that was on a good day!

As you might have noticed, Egyptian gods didn't look like friendly old bearded men sitting on clouds. No ... they were more like the scary things that live under your bed – monsters with the heads of animals, horns, wings and claws!

When gods look like that, you don't want to make them angry!

Grrrr! Grrrr!!

700 GODS

The only person allowed to talk to a god was the Pharaoh. This made him really powerful – if you didn't do what the Pharaoh asked, he wouldn't just put you in jail, he could ask the gods to strike you with lightning or make all your crops fail so your family would starve to death.

But it also meant the Pharaoh had a lot of responsibility. His main job was to make sure the gods were happy so they'd give Egypt good harvests and plenty of food. Because if things went wrong, guess who got the blame? You got it – the Pharaoh!

He was supposed to be the chief priest of all the gods in Egypt, which meant looking after over 700 gods, but to do that properly would have meant spending 25 hours a day running round from temple to temple making offerings to each one. It was impossible!

So instead, he chose an army of priests to do the job for him.

BABYSITTING A GOD

The gods were really important to the ancient Egyptians, so you won't be surprised to know that the places they lived in were pretty fabulous.

Some gods' temples were a bit like Buckingham Palace, with lots of posh rooms – including kitchens and dining rooms for feeding the god, and rooms to store the god's clothes and jewellery.

Outside you'd often find great pointed towers of stone called **obelisks**, usually put up by a Pharaoh who wanted to show that he'd won some big battle.

They weighed hundreds of tons and stood up to twenty metres high. No one knows exactly how the Egyptians managed to stand them up – although it probably involved some sort of ramp and a lot of ropes.

There aren't many obelisks left standing in Egypt – they were so popular that a lot of them were nicked and put up in cities around the world. Today you can spot Egyptian obelisks in Rome, Istanbul, New York and Paris! There's one called Cleopatra's Needle, which is near Waterloo Bridge in London, one in Durham, one in Dorset and a pair at the British Museum.

So what did you have to do if you were a priest? Well, apart from scrubbing your body in cold water and shaving your eyebrows, you were also supposed to have a clean mind – you had to promise not to lie or accept bribes or tell anyone what really went on in the temple. It was a bit like being in a secret club.

But your main job was to look after your particular god – which meant cleaning and dressing his statue, making offerings of food and drink to him and singing him songs about how great he was.

Babysitting a statue might seem like a pretty thankless task but the Pharaoh gave the temples lots of money and land to make sure the gods were properly looked after. So if you were a priest you could become very rich and powerful.

You also got nice food (you could scoff all the grub the statue didn't eat), a big temple to live in, you didn't have to fight when there was a war, AND you didn't have to pay taxes.

In fact it was such a cushy job that Pharaohs often chose members of their family to be priests.

Over time some priests became even more powerful than the Pharaoh – they said that they were the only people who understood what the gods were talking about and so the Pharaoh should obey them! Bet he wished he hadn't given them the job.

WHY DID GODS LOOK SO WEIRD?

Suppose a Pharaoh asked you to create a picture of a god of football.

Well, you might just cut out a photo of Wayne Rooney, but you probably wouldn't because he's got such a daft face.

So instead you might give your god a head like a football (so everyone would know what sort of god he was), a number nine on his shirt (so everyone knew he was a striker) and an engine on his back (because he powered his way past the opposition). You might even have a load of saliva coming out of his mouth (because he was good at dribbling). So he might not look very pretty, but your god would look pretty terrifying, and anyone who knew anything about football would know exactly what you were trying to say about him.

Turn the page to see how the Egyptians drew their gods.

The goddess **Tauert** had the head and body of a pregnant hippo. This was because she was the goddess of motherhood. Every Egyptian knew that if you got between a mother hippo and her young, there'd be trouble!

Ra was the sun god, so he was pictured with the sun on his head. But he also had the face of a falcon, because they're such fast, strong, fantastic-looking birds.

Anubis guarded the Underworld, but he had a jackal's face, probably because jackals often hung around cemeteries sniffing the graves.

Thoth was the god of writing, with the face of a bird called an ibis with a long curved beak. Some people think this is because the ibis is a sensible bird that never drinks stagnant water.

Sobek was the god of the great River Nile. It's full of crocodiles – so he had a croc's head.

Bes was an ugly little bearded dwarf. He looks a bit like a very small lion, so his looks may have been useful for scaring off evil spirits.

WHY ONE GOD HAD A GREEN FACE

One of the most popular gods was Osiris. He had two jobs. He was god of the harvest. But he was also the god of the Underworld (where Egyptians believed you went after you died), so he was pictured as a mummified Pharaoh with a green face.

He was supposed to have been a King of Egypt before being murdered by his brother Seth, the god of the desert. His body was cut up into lots of bits and spread across Egypt. His wife, Isis, tried to put him together again like a jigsaw, and bring him back to life, and she didn't do too badly. But just before she'd finished she realized she'd lost his willy and had to make him a new one out of solid gold!

But because he'd been killed he couldn't go back to being King of Egypt, so he became King of the Underworld.

Egyptians liked the story of Isis and Osiris because it was about things dying and coming back to life. In a way this is what happened every year in Egypt – when the desert sun baked everything to a crisp and then the Nile flooded and brought everything back to life!

TOO MANY FROGS

Egypt pops up in the Bible quite a bit. Which isn't surprising really, because the people who wrote it were from the place next door, the kingdom of Israel.

In one of the Bible's most famous stories, the prophet Moses leads the Jewish people (or 'Hebrews') out of Egypt. The story goes that there had been thousands of Hebrews there who were being forced to work as slaves, and Moses was told by God to free them.

The Pharaoh refused to let them leave, so God set ten plagues on Egypt (including plagues of **frogs**, **flies**, **locusts**, boils, thunder, hail, darkness and water turning to blood) and eventually the Pharaoh agreed to let the Hebrews go . . .

Moses then led the Hebrews across the Red Sea (getting God to part the waters so they could walk across it) and on an incredibly long walk through the desert until they finally settled in Canaan – or 'Israel' as they named it.

Unfortunately we don't know how much of the story is true – Egyptian records don't mention it and there's no other evidence anywhere of Moses or the 'ten plagues'.

But it shows how important Egypt was at the time the Bible was written. The Israelites believed they had escaped from there with God's help – as far as they were concerned this meant their God was stronger than all the Egyptian gods put together – green-faced Osiris, hippo-faced Tauert, bird-faced Thoth and even ugly little Bes.

Yuk! If I'd have been Moses, I'd have given in after the frogs.

ALIVE WHEN YOU'RE DEAD

What do you think will happen to you when you're dead?

For the ancient Egyptians it was the start of their 'afterlife'!

The afterlife was where you went after you died – in the afterlife you did all the things you did in life, but without all the hassle. Plus, you got to hang out with your dead ancestors (who'd probably just moan to you about how much better things were when they were alive).

At first only Pharaohs got an afterlife, but then ordinary Egyptians started to believe they could have one too – and they spent lots of time and money preparing for it.

They were very careful to make sure they took everything they were going to need – it was a bit like going on a very long holiday.

In order to have a really good afterlife, you packed your furniture, your clothes, your favourite food and your favourite pet. But you also needed a tomb to put it all in . . . and you had to have your body.

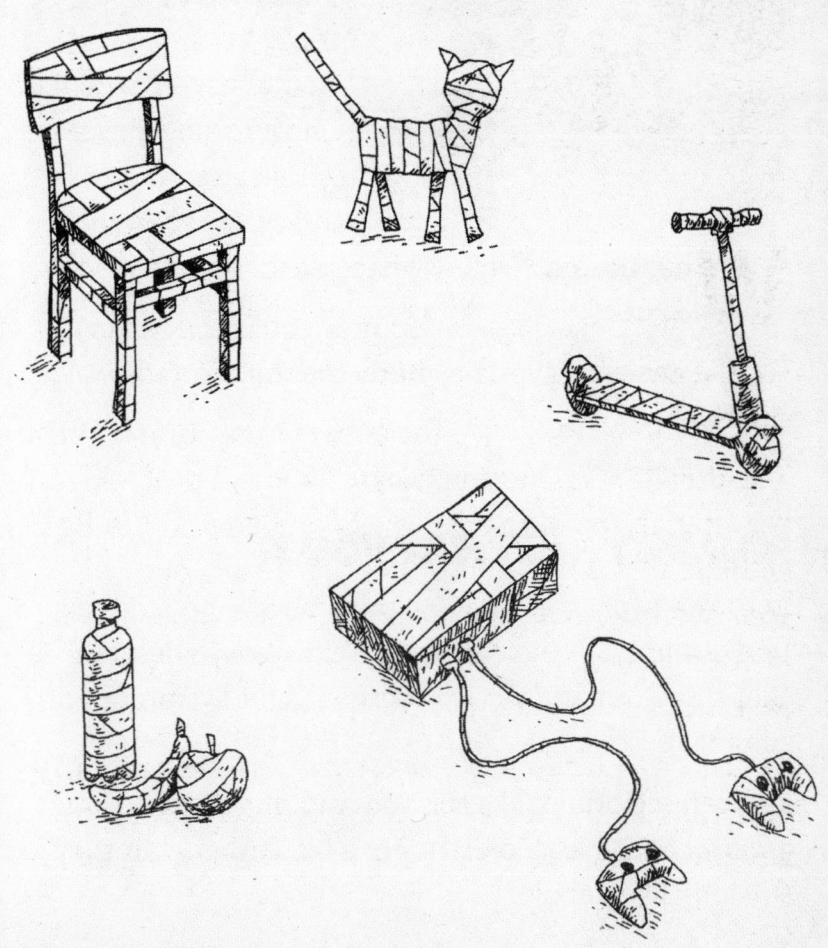

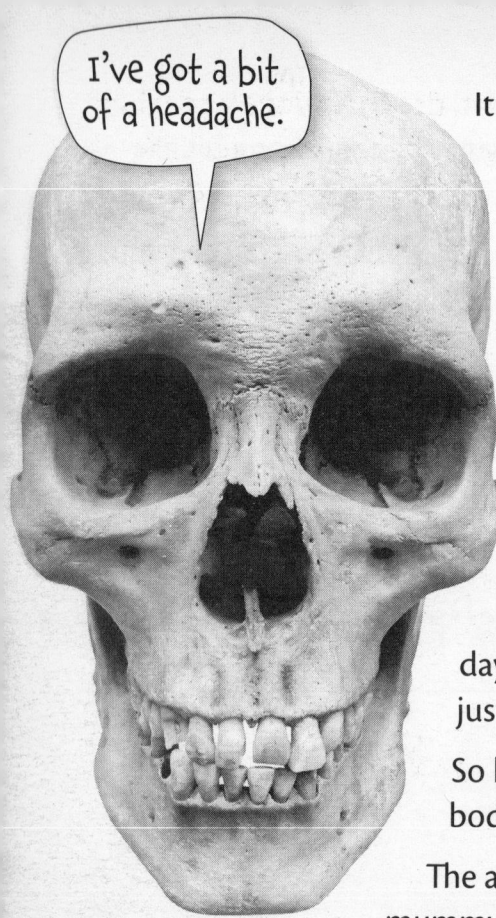

I've got a bit of a headache.

It might seem odd to us that the dead needed their bodies but the Egyptians believed that even in the afterlife, a person's spirit needed a body to live in.

This could be a bit tricky because dead bodies decompose – which means they start to stink after four or five days and pretty soon they're just a pile of bones.

So how could you live in a body that had rotted away?

The answer was – turn it into a mummy.

MUMMY - IS THAT YOU?

In the early days, ancient Egyptian people noticed that bodies buried in the desert didn't rot away – instead they dried out and were preserved (a bit like prunes or sultanas).

You can see bodies like this today in museums – some are over 5,000 years old; they're a bit leathery but they still look like people.

But this only happens in hot, dry conditions, and when the Egyptians started burying the dead in cold, dark tombs, they had to find another way to preserve their bodies. It was called 'mummification'.

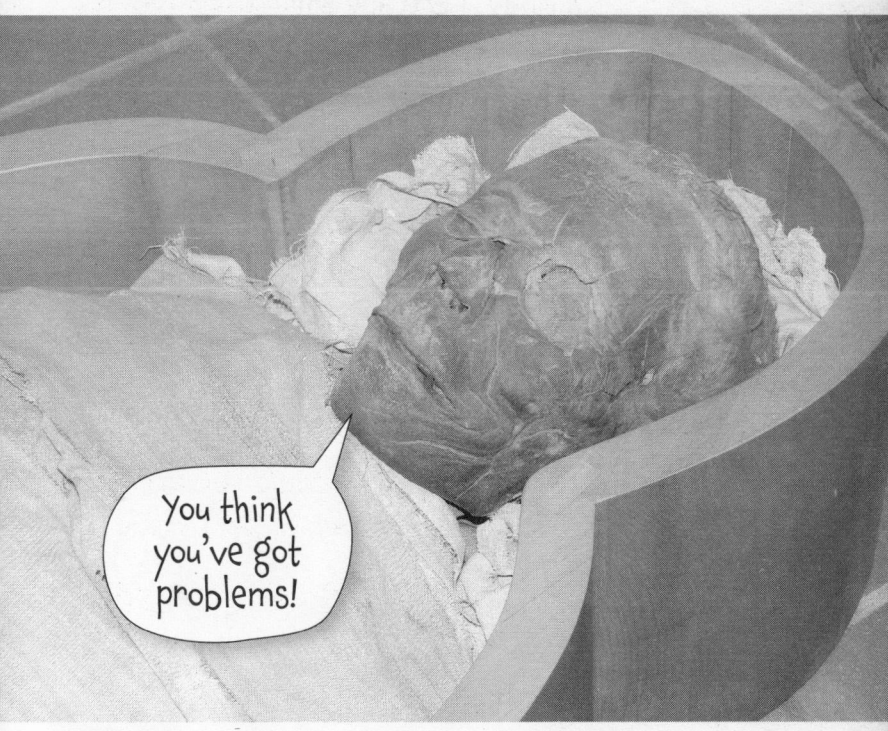

You think you've got problems!

Warning: if you're a bit squeamish and don't like hearing about really gross things, best to skip the next bit, although you've just read about dead bodies being like giant prunes, so you can't be that much of a wimp!

GRACE'S GUIDE TO MAKING A MUMMY

It could take up to 70 days to mummify a body. Here are the instructions.

1 First the body was cut open and all the sloppy bits like the liver, lungs, stomach and intestines were taken out and put into special jars.

2 Then a long metal hook was used to pull the brain out through the nose.

Squelch

3 Then the body was dried out using a salty substance called 'natron' which sucked up all its moisture. This took several weeks.

4 The head and body were then stuffed with sawdust and padding to stop them looking too shrivelled.

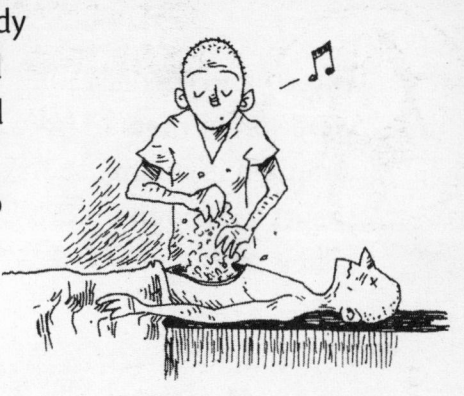

5 The eyeballs were pushed back into their sockets and covered with linen pads. Often these pads had eyes painted on them or sometimes the person's eyes were replaced with onions!

6 Onion-skin, wax or peppercorns were used to block up the nostrils.

7 Finger- and toenails were sometimes wrapped in metal sheets to stop them falling off.

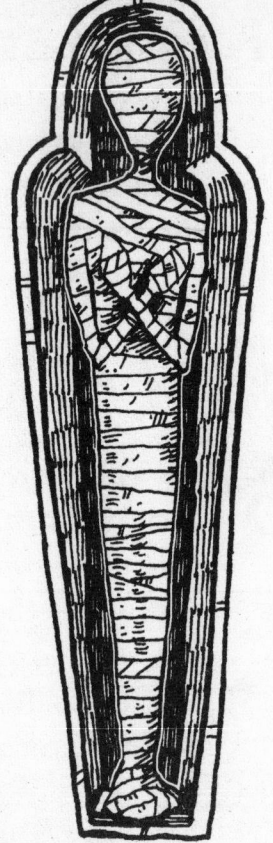

8 Finally the body was wrapped tightly in strips of linen, coated in a glue-like tree resin or plaster and put in a coffin.

WHEN A NAME STICKS

Did you know: the word 'mummy' comes from 'mummia' – the Persian word for 'tar' – because over time the resin used to coat the body turned black and sticky like tar.

WHO'S THE DADDY?

People have always wanted to unwrap mummies to see what's inside them. But mummies don't much like being undressed – once you've taken them apart, it's hard to put them back together again, because they've usually collapsed in bits.

So since the 1960s, experts have used X-rays and hi-tech scanning to examine mummies. This has helped them find out all about who or what's inside without causing any damage.

For instance, a female mummy from Birmingham Museum was scanned and found to be a man . . . you could say he was actually a daddy!

Mind you, not everybody received this top-of the-range treatment!

If you were poor, you got a rush job with none of the extras – no false eyeballs, no peppercorns up your nose, and no head stuffed with sawdust. The rich get all the fun, don't they?

MONKEY MUMMIES

The Egyptians didn't just mummify humans. Sometimes they mummified their cats and dogs so they could go into the afterlife too.

But it wasn't just their pets that got the mummy treatment. Thousands of wild animals, like crocodiles, snakes and even fish, were mummified as offerings to the gods. You'd pop down to your local temple, pay for an animal to be mummified and offer it to your favourite god as a kind of gift. The Egyptians had some very odd ideas about presents!

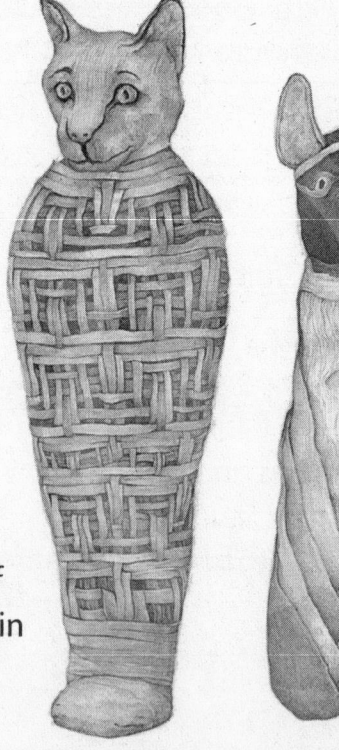

These gifts were so popular that sometimes the Egyptians ran out of animals to mummify. So the mummy makers made fake animal mummies instead and flogged them to worshippers who were too stupid to tell the difference between a dead cat and a bundle of sticks and rags wrapped in cloth.

RECYCLING MUMMY

Since ancient times people have believed Egyptian mummies have special properties, so they've dug them up and used them for all sorts of things . . .

MUMMY MEDICINE – Before there were medicines like aspirin and vitamin C, powdered mummy was thought to cure lots of illnesses. In the sixteenth century, King Francis I of France was said to take a dose of powdered mummy with rhubarb every day!

MUMMY PAINT – Artists in the sixteenth and seventeenth centuries used a sludgy paint called 'Egyptian Brown' – made from powdered mummy bits!

MUMMY FERTILIZER – In the 1800s, thousands of mummified cats were mashed up and turned into fertilizer.

MUMMY PARTIES – In the 1840s and 1850s, mummy-unwrapping parties were popular in Europe. People came round to your house to unwrap a mummy, followed by drinks and nibbles.

Once your body had been mummified, it needed to be put somewhere safe – in other words, you needed a tomb . . .

HOW TO HIDE YOUR MUMMY

You may remember that the Egyptians eventually stopped burying their Pharaohs' mummies in pyramids because they kept getting robbed. Instead they decided it was much cleverer to bury them in a secret location.

They chose a valley in the hills outside Thebes (near modern-day Luxor) and started building hidden tombs cut deep into the rocky valley sides. For 500 years, Pharaohs and their families were buried here – it became known as the **Valley of the Kings**.

You're probably asking, '*If it was a secret, how come we know where it is?*' Well, the truth is that the ancient Egyptians weren't very good at keeping quiet.

Within a couple of centuries lots of people knew where the Valley of the Kings was, and I expect you can guess what happened next . . .

Yes – tomb robbers came along and cleared out all the tombs!

Those pesky tomb robbers got everywhere . . .

Are you sure this is Swindon?

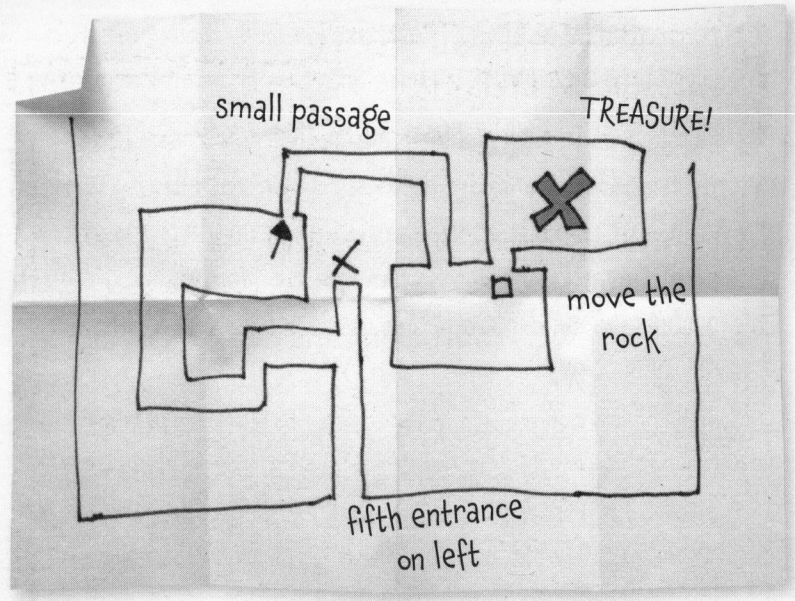

small passage

TREASURE!

move the rock

fifth entrance on left

In fact it's a bit suspicious when you think about it . . . How come so many tombs got discovered and robbed when so much effort had been made to hide them?

It turns out that a lot of the thieves were the workers who'd helped to build the tombs in the first place! We know this because some of them got caught and were put on trial, and confessed.

Robbing a Pharaoh, even a dead one, was a very serious crime. Convicted criminals were beaten and sometimes had their hands, tongue, nose or ears cut off before being impaled on a stake, burned alive or tied up in a sack and thrown in the Nile – I'd rather have got an ASBO, wouldn't you?

PACKING FOR ETERNITY

People used to pack so much stuff in their tombs that there wasn't enough room for everything.

So they started making little models of all the things they needed – tools, weapons, furniture, boats, houses and gardens – and then put them in their tomb instead of the real thing.

They even put in models of their servants baking bread and brewing beer, farmers ploughing fields, carpenters making furniture and weavers weaving cloth – so they could spend the afterlife chilling out while the models did all the work for them.

Don't you wish you had your own clay person to do your homework and clean your room?

BOOK OF THE DEAD

So you've got your mummy and a tomb full of stuff – that's you sorted for the afterlife then?

Well . . . no, not exactly. Not everyone got in. You had to know the right passwords and magic spells.

These were written in a special guidebook called the *Book of the Dead*.

It also showed the tests you had to pass. The most important one was the weighing of your heart. When you died it would be weighed on some scales and if it was lighter than a feather you could pass on to the afterlife. But if it was heavy with sin, it would be eaten by a demon and you wouldn't be allowed in.

Yum!

SIDEWAYS PEOPLE

You might have noticed that Egyptian tomb paintings can seem a bit strange – everyone is looking sideways and standing funny. Some people are bigger than others and there are lots of odd symbols floating around them.

Artists in Egypt had to follow strict rules when they painted pictures:

- People were always drawn so you could see as much as possible of the body – with both arms and legs showing, but their face sideways to show their profile (so you could also see their nose).

- Men were always painted with dark red skin and women with lighter skin.

- The more important the person, the larger they appeared in the picture. Pharaohs and gods were the biggest, while servants and slaves were teeny!

Anyone fancy a cupcake?

THE CURSE OF KING TUT'S TOMB

One tomb in the Valley of the Kings wasn't totally cleaned out by robbers.

It's the most famous, and it belonged to a boy who was only nine years old when he became Pharaoh and died before he was twenty.

His name was Tutankhamun but he's better known as King Tut.

In 1922 a team of Egyptologists led by Howard Carter discovered his tomb and to everyone's surprise, it still had a lot of his stuff in it.

In fact, like a typical teenager's bedroom today, it was a jumbled mess. Over 3,500 objects were piled up in it, from furniture and clothing to archery equipment and musical instruments.

Most importantly it contained his mummified body and an incredible solid-gold death mask inlaid with precious stones.

King Tut didn't live very long and he wasn't a very successful Pharaoh, but his tomb was the find of the century!

And there's another spookier reason why Tut is so famous . . .

Soon after the discovery, Lord Carnarvon who had funded the expedition suddenly dropped dead . . . **AAARGHH!**

Rumours quickly spread that the men who had opened Tut's tomb had become the victims of a terrible curse, and because they'd disturbed the Pharaoh's rest, they'd die a dreadful death too . . . **AAARGHH! AAARGHH!**

According to one newspaper, 25 people involved in discovering the Pharaoh's tomb died soon afterwards . . . **AAARGHH! AAARGHH! AAARGHH!**

Which proves one thing – you should never trust what you read in the papers.

The reality is, ten years after the discovery, only six people involved had died. Many more lived to a ripe old age – including Howard Carter, the man who had led the expedition! If there was a curse, it wasn't very effective. Lord Carnarvon had been killed by something much less dramatic – an infected mosquito bite!

AAARGHH! AAARGHH! AAARGHH! AAARGHH!

HIEROGLYPHS

The Egyptians didn't just speak a different language to us, they wrote words in a completely different way! They didn't use letters like we do. They used a system of pictures called **hieroglyphs**.

'Hieroglyph' means 'holy writing' – because it was developed by Egyptian priests to write on temples and tombs.

At first they just drew pictures of objects –

~~~~ = water   = old man   = tree   = fish

A picture of a sheep with five lines would mean five sheep.

Sounds easy? Well it's not . . . Otherwise it wouldn't have taken the experts twenty years to work it out.

Over time hieroglyphs got more complicated. Each word was broken down into sounds (like we break words up into letters) and each sound given its own symbol.

For example, the Egyptian word for 'cat' was 'meiw'. So they wrote it out like this and just to help make it clear what they meant, they put a picture of a cat at the end:

Me   i   w

When the scribes wrote everyday things like letters and receipts, they didn't spend hours painstakingly drawing and colouring in each little picture. They scribbled a quick version of the symbol, which is just a load of little squiggles and is even harder to read.

And if this wasn't confusing enough, hieroglyphics can be read from right to left, left to right or up and down (depending on which way all the animals are facing) . . .

Nits?! She must be here somewhere.

GRUESOME STUFF

So was ancient Egypt a really peaceful place, full of happy, friendly people who worshipped weird little dwarfs, made model servants and got together to build pyramids?

PARTLY, YES ... The Egyptians didn't go charging around the world conquering lots of foreign lands like other ancient civilizations did. They couldn't see the point – they had virtually everything they needed at home. And the Pharaoh and his mates were so rich that if there were a few top-of-the-range luxury goods they didn't have, they could go and buy them in some other country.

BUT PARTLY, NO! You don't get to be a global superpower by being a pushover. And sometimes they got really stroppy.

THREE REASONS THE ANCIENT EGYPTIANS GOT STROPPY

1 Foreign places sometimes stopped selling Egypt fancy top-of-the-range stuff because they'd been invaded by other countries who'd taken all the  good stuff for themselves. When this happened, the Pharaoh would get a bit cross (in other words completely mental), and lots of people would end up dead.

2 By and large, Egypt was a pretty cool place to live, with lots of food to eat and plenty of land to farm, so people from other countries kept moving in. This was fine until they tried to take Egypt over and run it themselves. When this happened even more people ended up dead!

3 If anything went seriously wrong in Egypt and people started to blame the Pharaoh, he'd order his army to attack foreign lands just to prove he was the most brilliant fighter in the world, and that everyone ought to give him more respect. When this happened, guess what . . . The undertakers got really rich.

So all in all, the Egyptians did a fair bit of killing for a 'peaceful' people.

This way to the afterlife. Make yourselves at home.

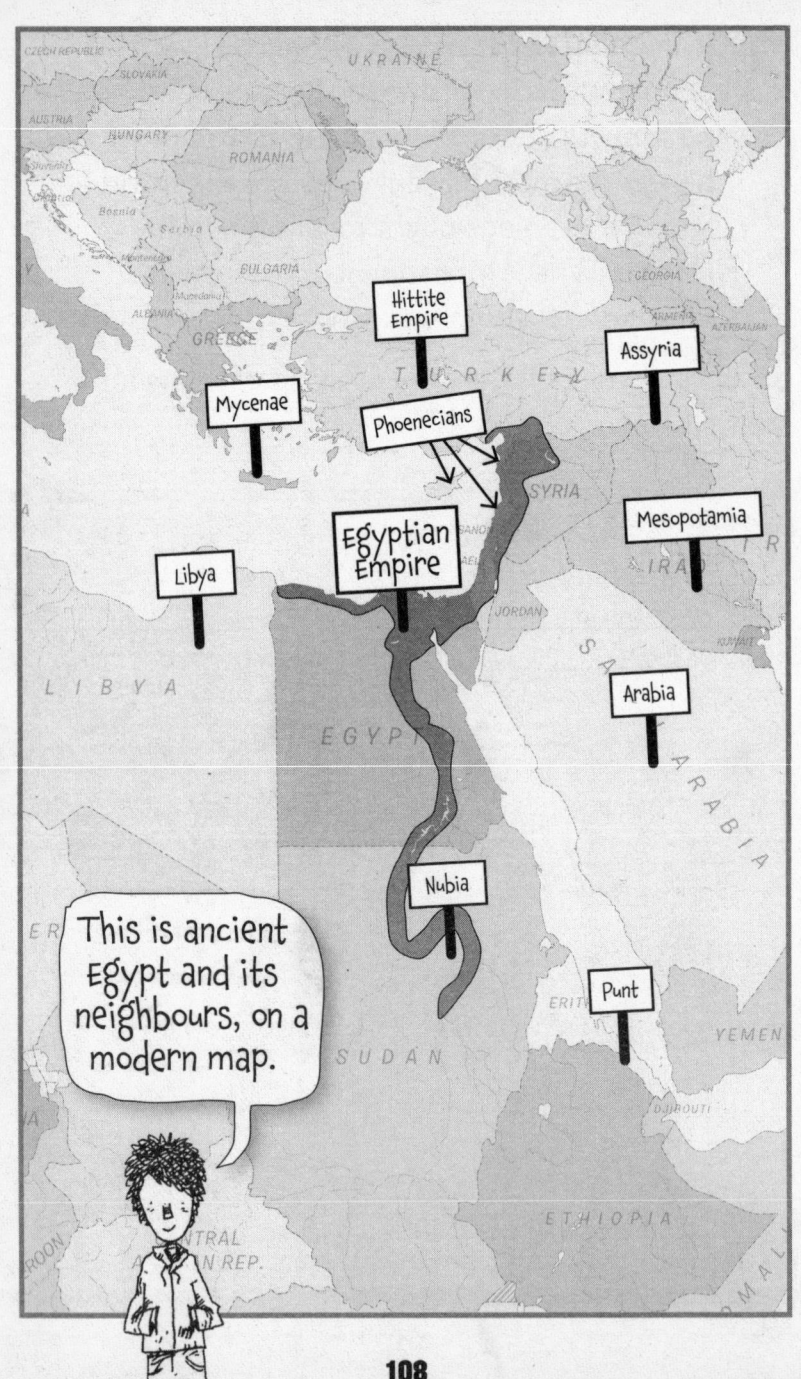

BULLY YOUR NEIGHBOUR

Often a country's main enemy is its next-door neighbour – the people who live just across the river, or on the other side of the nearest mountain.

It's like fighting with your brother or sister – they're always in your face and when you're in a bad mood they're a convenient person to hit.

The Egyptians were no exception. They didn't have many neighbours – to the north was the Mediterranean Sea, to the east the Red Sea and to the west the Sahara Desert. But to the south lay the land of Nubia. Lucky Nubians . . .

Nubia was the place Egyptians went for their gold, and because they wanted control of the gold, they decided to control Nubia.

It was easy to beat the Nubians because they were quite poor and there weren't many of them. So if a Pharaoh wanted to look good and didn't have anyone else to fight, he'd send troops into Nubia to wallop the locals, come back with tales of victory, and maybe pick up some more gold while they were at it.

DIRTY FIGHTERS

In 1897 a piece of stone was found near a temple in the Egyptian desert. It shows a pretty grim sight. A Pharaoh is clutching the hair on an enemy soldier's head with one hand, and in the other he's got a club with which he's about to clobber the man. Just below him, two dead bodies are floating in the water.

This carving is from Egypt's early days. So we can be pretty sure that right from the beginning, the Egyptians were boasting about how aggressive they were on the battlefield.

You're not a nice man.

PEEWEE'S SHORT HISTORY OF STICKS

The Egyptians thought sticks were very useful weapons.

Sticks are cheap, easy to find and you didn't need any training apart from your sergeant saying, 'See this stick? Whack someone with it!'

As time went by, though, they stopped using ordinary sticks and made them more complicated and ferocious.

For instance they developed . . .

The Throwing Stick:
It's a stick . . . that you throw.

The Throwing Spear: A
stick with a pointy bit on the end – so when you throw it, it doesn't just bounce off your enemy, it sticks in!

111

The Mace: A stick with a stone on the end of it. Capable of breaking bones, and crushing a skull like the top of a boiled egg.

The Battle Axe: Similar to the above but using a stone with a sharp edge so you can also chop arms and legs off.

The Bow and Arrow: A bendy stick with a string, which fires a straight stick with a pointy bit on the end.

SOLDIERS IN SKIRTS

So what protection did the brave soldier have against such a dazzling array of sticks?

Not a lot! For most of Egyptian history soldiers wore no body armour at all. It might sound crazy to dress in not much more than a skirt, and then go into battle with all those sticks flying about, but it was for a good reason.

Ever tried picking up a metal coin that's been sitting in the sun?

In the desert heat, any armour – especially metal armour – would quickly have got really hot and the soldiers would have been roasted alive before they arrived on the battlefield.

But they were given big shields to hide behind, especially once their enemies got better at making metal objects, and sticks were replaced by weapons like daggers and swords.

NEIGHBOURS FROM HELL

Between 1800 and 1650 BC, the Nile delta slowly filled up with foreigners from the east. The Egyptians called them the 'Hyksos' and there were so many of them that they formed their own kingdom in the north of Egypt. What a cheek!

If that wasn't bad enough, they deliberately started to annoy the Egyptians. Their king even sent a letter to the Pharaoh demanding that he drain his hippo pool because the noise of the hippos was keeping him awake at night!

Pretty soon the two kingdoms were kicking lumps out of each other. The Pharaoh, Seqenere Tao II, was probably killed in a battle with the Hyksos. How do we know? Well, his mummy was examined and it shows a massive slash across his forehead caused by a type of axe used by the Hyksos.

The Pharaohs eventually drove the Hyksos out of Egypt. But not before the Egyptians had picked up some tricks and tips from them about fighting battles.

The most important of these was how to use a **horse-drawn chariot**.

FIVE FERRARIS

Horses and chariots were new to the Egyptians – the first Egyptian to see one in action was probably dumb-struck. But not for long: within seconds he'd have been running for the nearest shelter ducking the arrows whizzing past his head.

With chariots, battles became faster and more sudden. Groups of charging chariots carrying archers could break through enemy lines, encircle the enemy troops and chase down anyone trying to run away.

The chariot was like the sports car of the ancient world. Pharaohs used them as status symbols as well as in battle. When King Tut died six chariots were buried in his tomb – including a gold one . . . How cool is that?

It's a bit like being buried with five Ferraris and a golden Range Rover!

This bit is very gruesome.

No it isn't; it's very, very gruesome.

THE WORST JOB IN THE WORLD

Being a soldier in the Egyptian army was really hard, even for very young recruits. Children were brought to the army camps and virtually imprisoned there. They'd be punched in the body and the head until they were bleeding, in order to make them tough. Then they were thrown to the ground and stomped on. They had to go off on long marches carrying all their food and drink on their backs like donkeys, their water was polluted, and the only time they were allowed to stop was when it was their turn to go on guard duty.

After that, going into battle must have come as a bit of a relief.

Mind you, they needed to be tough. In battle they often sustained horrific injuries. A tomb containing the bodies of sixty Egyptian soldiers was excavated and showed that most had died from being hit on the head or punctured with arrows.

Without modern medicines, even a slight injury could be fatal. Dirt in the wound would quickly have led to infection and death.

Egyptian doctors could treat some things: they applied honey and other natural ointments to help clean wounds and put broken bones in splints. But often whether you lived or died was in the hands of the gods.

Twang

119

JOJO'S MEDICAL CURES –
EGYPTIAN STYLE

Baldness – Rub your head with a mixture of lion fat and various bits from a hippopotamus, crocodile, cat, snake and a big horned goat.

Grey Hair – Eat a mouse cooked in oil.

Whooping Cough – Eat a mouse roasted to a cinder and ground into a basin of milk.

Headache – Dab your head with the skull of a catfish fried in oil.

Infertility – Drink a mixture of dried, pounded dung-beetles in water.

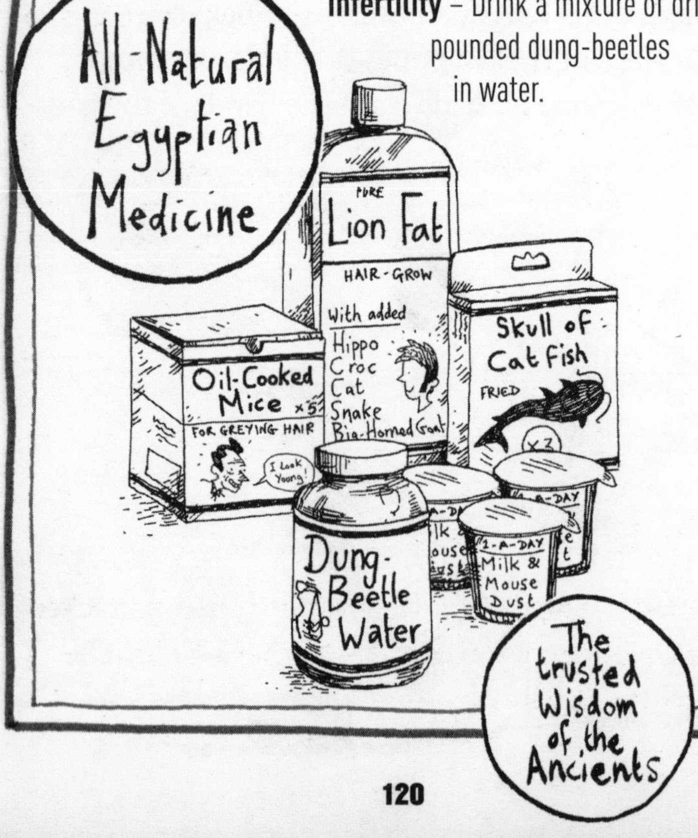

All-Natural Egyptian Medicine

PURE
Lion Fat
HAIR - GROW
With added
Hippo
Croc
Cat
Snake
Big-Horned Goat

Skull of Cat Fish
FRIED
x 2

Oil-Cooked Mice x5
FOR GREYING HAIR
I look Young!

Dung-Beetle Water

2-A-DAY
Milk & Mouse Dust

The trusted Wisdom of the Ancients

But if you were lucky enough to survive, the rewards could be huge. Plunder was a perk of the job. The winning army got to take anything they wanted – who was going to stop them? So soldiers scoured the battlefield for shiny stuff to take home, plus they might be given a prisoner or two to keep as slaves.

GET RICH QUICK

Pharaohs soon realized that winning a war or two was a quick way to get filthy rich.

Not only did you get loads of booty, but the losing country had to pay a huge fine to Egypt every year in the form of luxury goods (which was why Pharaoh and his mates had so many of them).

What's booty?

I think it's shoes for a baby.

And other countries that were afraid of being attacked by the Egyptians *also* paid them so they wouldn't be invaded. It was win-win.

LOTS OF LOOT

After the Battle of Megiddo (around 1480 BC), the booty taken home by the victorious Egyptian army included 340 prisoners, 2,238 horses, 924 chariots, 200 suits of armour, 1,929 cows, 22,500 sheep, 87 knives, three kettles, and the King of Megiddo's tent poles.

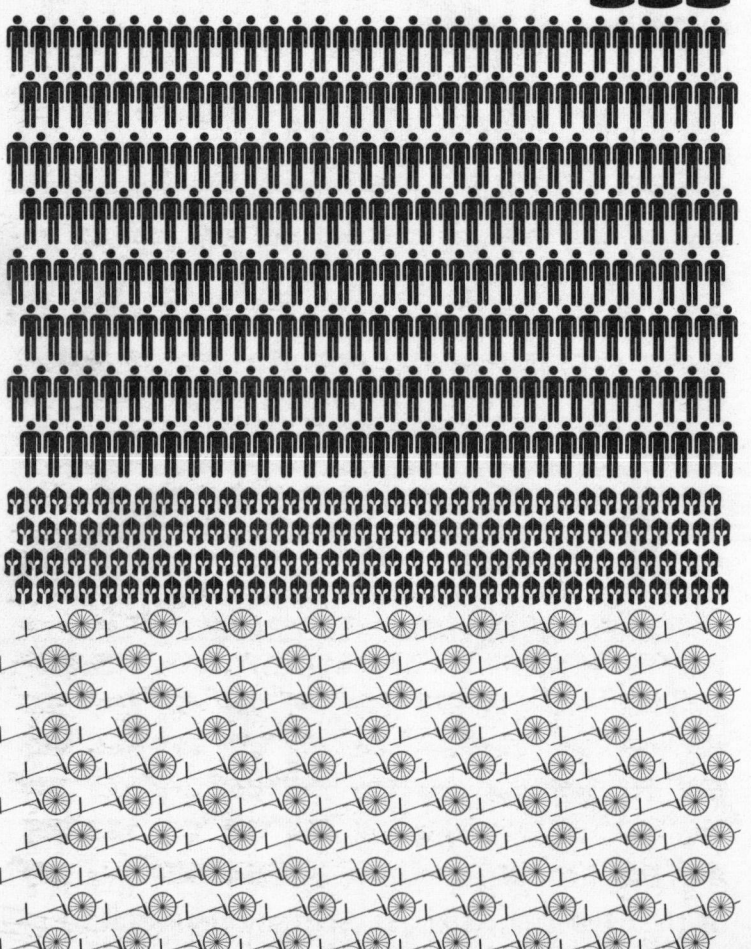

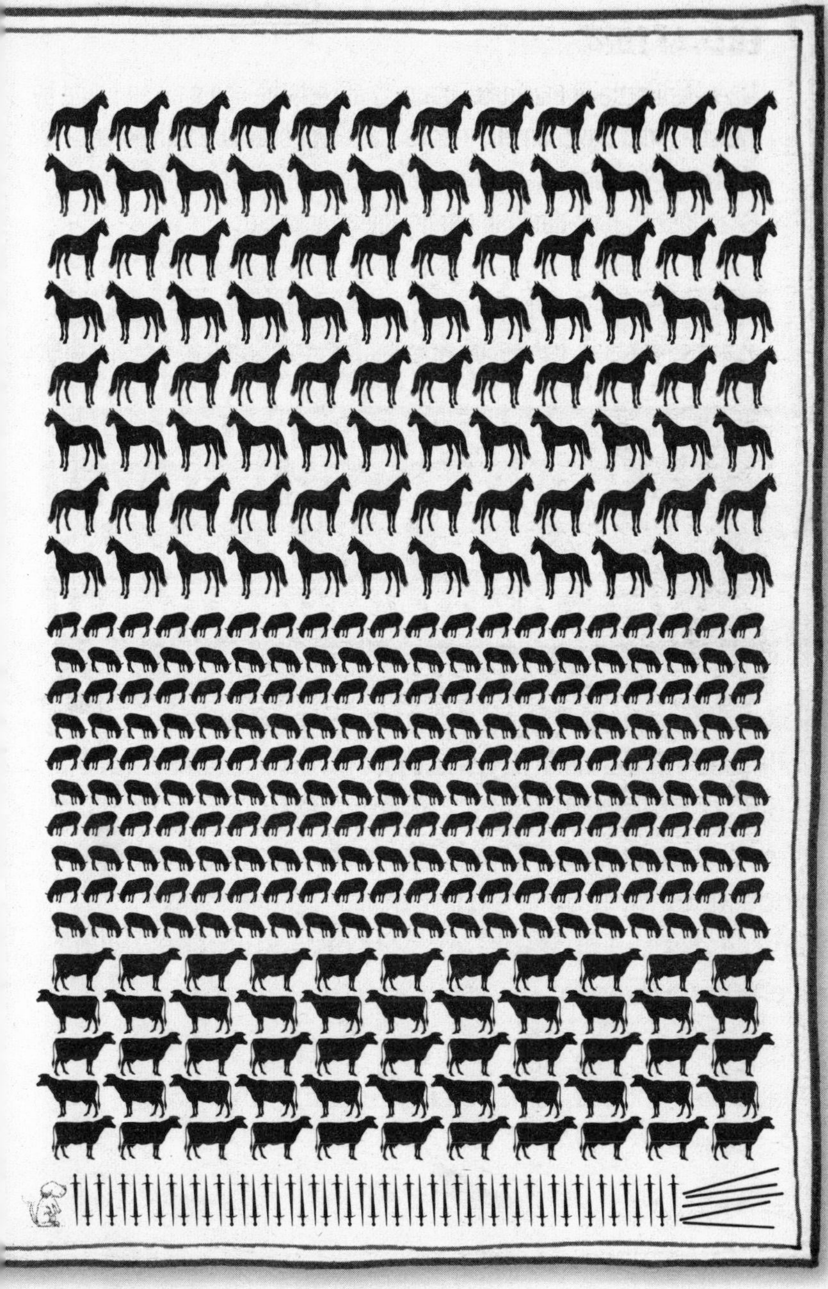

EGG-TASTIC TRIBUTES

These fines, called **tribute**, came in all forms – from precious metals to timber and cattle. Sometimes countries also sent weird animals. The royal records of Pharaoh Thutmose III included something the Egyptians got really excited about – four strange birds that laid eggs every day . . . You'd have thought everyone would have known about chickens – but apparently the Egyptians didn't!!

So what happened to all the money the Pharaoh collected? Did every Egyptian get given a free chariot? Did all the old people get a holiday by the sea? Did every kid get a huge surprise present on their birthday? Nope! It all went on huge pyramids, palaces and temples for the Pharaoh, and lots of monuments telling everyone how great he was!

Everywhere you went there were carvings of a giant Pharaoh clobbering the enemy or trampling over piles of dead bodies.

But even if a Pharaoh didn't actually win a battle, it didn't stop him claiming he had.

The great Pharaoh Rameses II led an army to recapture the city of Kadesh. Afterwards, an account of the battle was put up in temples all over Egypt – pictures show a large confused mass of Kadeshites being trampled to the ground by Egyptians.

Only thing is – Rameses didn't actually win the battle and he didn't recover Kadesh. But why stop a little thing like the truth getting in the way of a good picture?

GET THE MESSAGE?

Stone slabs have been found from the time when Pharaoh Amenhotep II crushed a rebellion in Syria. He obviously wanted to send a tough message to anyone who might think about defying Egypt, because one at Karnak shows lots of prisoners tied up and being paraded in front of Amenhotep.

Another found in Nubia says that the victorious Pharaoh then sailed back up the Nile with seven captured Syrian princes tied upside down from the bows of his royal barge! His prisoners were then escorted to a nearby temple and executed. Six of their headless bodies were placed on the walls of the temple. The seventh was taken to Nubia and put on display there – just in case the Nubians were thinking of trying anything similar.

Can you give me a hand?

Sorry, I'm tied up at the moment.

GIVE US A HAND

Heaps of severed hands were often shown in victory pictures to illustrate the number of people killed. Hands were useful. They could be cut off the dead and taken away to be counted up later.

But the Egyptians cheated. They didn't count the hands of their own dead – just those of the enemy. That way they always came out the winners!

PUSHY PERSIANS

It was probably only a matter of time before an Empire came along that was more powerful than Egypt.

The Persians came from what we now call Iran in the Middle East. Unlike Egypt, they were an Empire built on conquest – they wanted other people's land and were prepared to use military force to get it.

Egypt was an obvious target and eventually the Persian Emperor Cambyses II invaded and took control of the Egyptian capital city, Memphis.

Push off, bossyboots!

Cambyses was now the new Pharaoh and Egypt became part of the Persian Empire.

For many ordinary Egyptians not a lot changed at first – they kept farming the land, feeding the kids and building their tombs.

But there was no getting away from the fact that Egypt was being ruled by foreigners – from now on it would be the Egyptians who would have to pay tribute and do what they were told, or face being crushed by the stroppy Persian army!

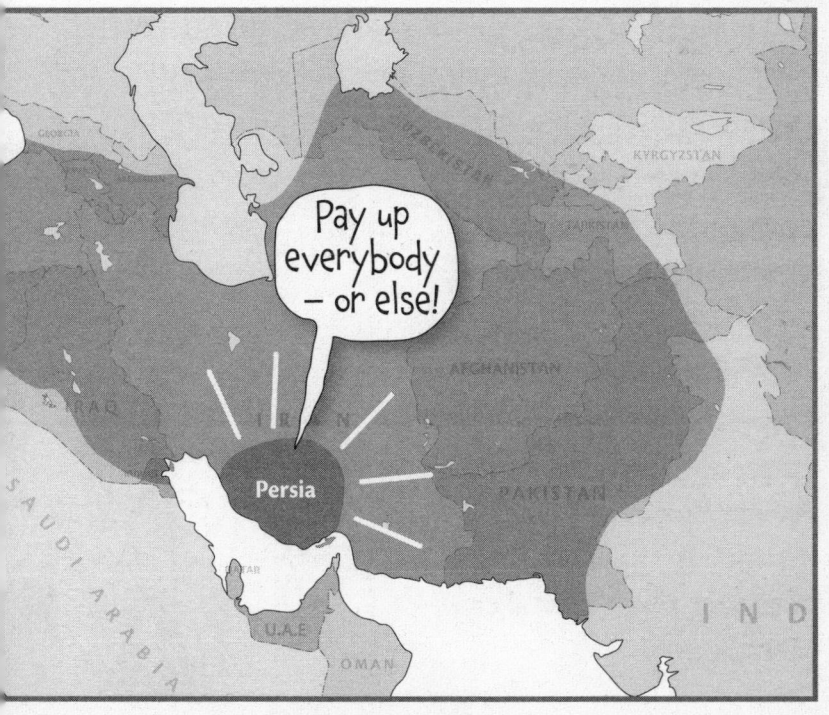

EGYPTOMANIA

Since you began reading this book you may have noticed that you've started dreaming of pyramids, nagging your parents to let you take a long holiday to Egypt, or wanting to mummify your goldfish.

If so, you're suffering from a severe case of **Egyptomania**.

Don't worry – it's not fatal!

Lots of people in history have had Egyptomania – from Greek writers to Roman Emperors and Victorian explorers. They went on long voyages to see the pyramids, drew sketchbooks full of pictures of temples, and brought back casefuls of souvenirs; they decorated their homes and built their tombs in Egyptian style, and in general went absolutely bonkers about everything Egyptian.

I prefer home.

FLYING SNAKES

The world's first travel guide to Egypt was written way back in 450 BC by a Greek called Herodotus. He had Egyptomania. He said that Egypt had 'more wonders than any other country'.

I ♥ Egypt!

A lot of what he wrote was accurate but he didn't *always* get things right – for example, he said that Egypt was attacked every year by flying snakes, that the hippopotamus was an animal with a mane and tail, and that it neighed like a horse!

14 CITIES WITH THE SAME NAME

Egypt was so famously full of wonders that all through history, lots of people have wanted to conquer it. One such man was Alexander the Great.

In 336 BC he inherited the kingdom of Macedonia in Greece. But he wanted something a bit bigger and within thirteen years he'd conquered the entire Persian Empire, including Egypt . . . They didn't call him **Alexander the Great** for nothing. Well, actually, the Persians didn't call him 'Alexander the Great' at all . . . They called him 'Alexander the ✦❋✿❀❤!!' Not surprising really.

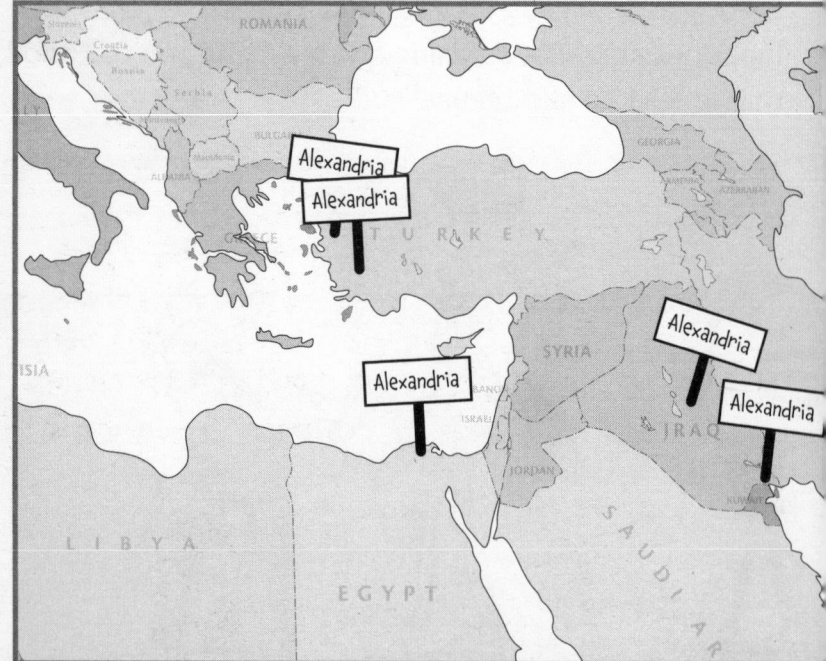

He only came to Egypt for a few weeks, but he immediately turned into a big fan of all things Egyptian. He was crowned Pharaoh in a big ceremony in its capital city, Memphis. His picture was carved on to temples and his name translated into Egyptian hieroglyphs.

Before he moved on to conquer other countries, he founded a new Egyptian city on the coast of the Mediterranean Sea and named it Alexandria. (Mind you, he loved founding cities and naming them after himself. In total, he founded **fourteen** cities called Alexandria.)

He may have been a military genius, but he wasn't very good at place names!

SNEAKY SOSTRATUS

Alexandria soon became a really busy place, with loads of tourists, business people and fancy goods coming to it from faraway places. So to help sailors find their way in and out of it at night, the ancient Egyptians decided they needed a lighthouse. But being Egyptians, they didn't want any old lighthouse – it had to be the biggest and the best in the entire world!

So they built a massive tower more than 100 metres tall and at the top they put a chamber with a fire inside that burned through the night. A mirror reflected the firelight for miles across the sea.

Travellers to Alexandria were so impressed that they named it a 'Wonder of the World'. So now Egypt had two wonders, the pyramids and the lighthouse, which must have made them feel very smug.

But the smuggest person of all was the man who built it – Sostratus. He was so pleased with himself that he wanted to write his name on it so everyone would remember him, but the Pharaoh refused to let him (only Pharaohs were allowed to write their names on things like that).

So Sostratus did something very sneaky and clever – he inscribed his name on the base of the building but then he covered it in a thin layer of plaster and chiselled Pharaoh's name on to it. Over time the plaster wore away to reveal the inscription beneath – Sostratus got his way after all!

15 PHARAOHS WITH THE SAME NAME

When Alexander died, his Empire was divided up and one of his trusted generals, called Ptolemy (pronounced **Tol-em-ee**), took control of Egypt.

He and his descendants are known as the **Ptolemies** because all the men in the family were called Ptolemy – Ptolemy the first, Ptolemy the second, Ptolemy the third . . . etc., etc. all the way up to Ptolemy the fifteenth!

Ptolemy (the first one) brought Alexander's mummified body to Egypt and put it in a tomb in Alexandria, where for centuries Greek and Roman visitors went to see it.

But that wasn't the only place they visited. The Greeks and Romans were just like us: they wanted to go to all the sites they'd read about, buy souvenirs and let everyone know where they'd been.

They even left graffiti all over some of Egypt's most famous monuments – including the tombs in the Valley of the Kings!

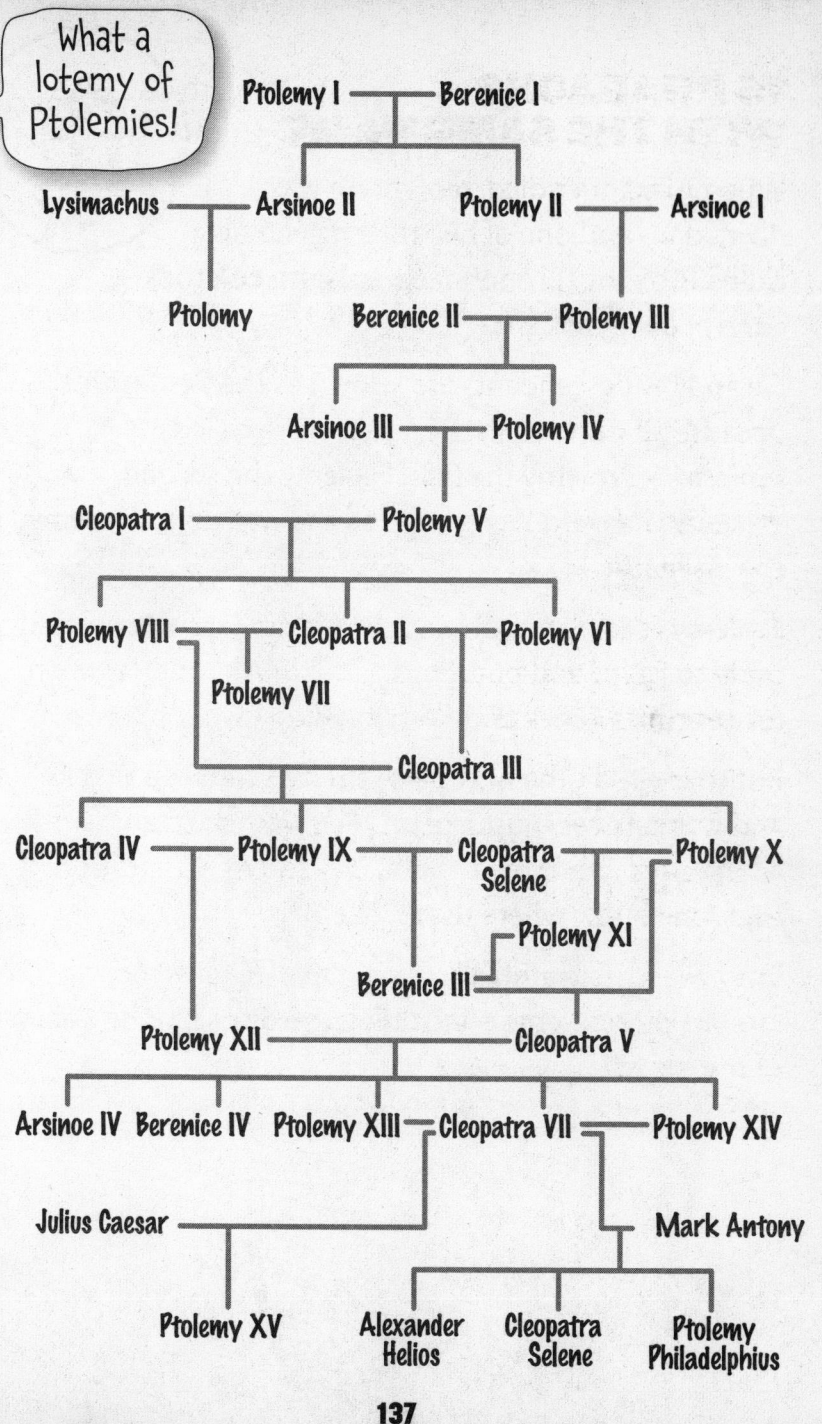

CAESAR WOZ 'ERE

Among the people who visited Alexander's tomb was the famous Roman ruler **Julius Caesar**.

He'd won lots of military victories and it looked as though Rome was going to become the next big superpower on the block. So the Egyptian Pharaohs knew they needed Roman support if they were going to be allowed to carry on being Pharaohs.

That's a bit like staying friends with the school bully to avoid being beaten to a pulp.

Caesar was in town because one of his enemies had fled to Egypt and he'd followed in hot pursuit. When he arrived, the Pharaoh (Ptolemy the thirteenth) presented him with the decapitated head of his enemy . . . which saved him a lot of trouble and probably gave him a bit more time for sightseeing.

SHAME ABOUT THE NOSE!

During his trip, Caesar met the Pharaoh's sister, the legendary **Cleopatra**, and they fell in love.

With Caesar's support, Cleopatra pushed her brother out of the way and became sole ruler of Egypt.

Legend has it that Cleopatra was one of the most beautiful women in the world, but coins from that time show her looking like a bloke with a big nose ...

If she was really like that, I can't see what all the fuss was about!

Unfortunately for Cleopatra, Caesar went back home and was quickly murdered. A big fight broke out over who would rule the Roman Empire next. The main contenders were a general called Mark Antony and Caesar's adopted son Octavian.

Mark Antony copped off with Cleopatra (maybe he liked big noses!), and joined forces with her against Octavian, but they were defeated in battle and Octavian invaded Egypt.

Unlike Caesar and Mark Antony, Octavian didn't fall for Cleopatra's nose. Instead he took her prisoner. Realizing she was beaten, Cleopatra killed herself – legend has it she allowed herself to be bitten by a poisonous snake.

After she died the Romans took over Egypt, so she was the very last Pharaoh.

141

TAKE HOME A CROCODILE

Octavian became Emperor of Rome, changed his name to 'Augustus' (or 'the exalted one') and Egypt became a province in the new Roman Empire . . .

It was known as the 'bread-basket' of Rome – huge shiploads of Egyptian grain were transported across the Mediterranean to feed the Roman army. But it wasn't just food that the Romans took back with them.

To ordinary Romans, Egypt was a land of exotic riches and they went crazy for Egyptian-style buildings, furniture and decoration. They built pyramid-style tombs and Romans living in Egypt even got themselves mummified!

In the second century AD the Roman Emperor Hadrian visited Egypt and was so impressed that he filled his villa back home with sculpted crocodiles, baboons, sphinxes and statues of Egyptian gods.

The Romans even adopted Egyptian gods like Isis and Osiris. They built new temples for them and imported 'holy water' from the Nile to use in their temple rituals.

ANCIENT EGYPT?
NEVER HEARD OF IT!

All this ended in the fourth century AD, when Christianity became the new religion of the Roman Empire.

Early Christians definitely weren't big fans of ancient Egypt.

Christianity banned the worship of other gods, so Christian Emperors shut down Egyptian temples and refused to allow anything connected with Egyptian religion – including Egyptian writing.

Which meant that, pretty soon, everyone forgot how to read hieroglyphics.

Over time, they forgot about ancient Egypt all together.

ANCIENT EGYPT
BACK IN THE CHARTS!

Until the eighteenth century hardly anyone bothered travelling to Egypt any more. Why would you go hundreds of miles to a sandpit in the middle of nowhere? Bor-ing!

Just about the only person interested in it was the French general Napoleon Bonaparte – and he wanted to invade it! But because he was so passionate about its history, he also arranged for a team of scientists, artists and mapmakers to come along and study the country's art and architecture.

Napoleon's invasion failed, but his team came back with lots of new information about Egypt and pictures of Egyptian art. A book was published describing what they'd found and quickly became a sell-out hit!

Among the bits and pieces his scientists brought back with them was a piece of stone covered in mysterious writing, which had been found in place called **Rosetta**.

The writing turned out to be the same passage written three times in different languages including Egyptian hieroglyphics and classical Greek.

Scholars used their knowledge of Greek to try to work out what the hieroglyphics meant.

For hundreds of years all signs and symbols written on the sides of the tombs and temples had seemed like gibberish, but now everyone could understand them. Once again ancient Egypt became all the rage.

THE CIRCUS STRONGMAN

Giovanni Belzoni was a strongman in a travelling circus who went to Egypt in 1815 to seek his fortune. His talent for lifting heavy things was put to use removing big bits of Egyptian statuary and shipping them to Britain for sale.

G. BELZONI.

Belzoni dragged this huge statue through the desert for two weeks . . . and now it's in the British Museum.

He travelled all over Egypt looking for treasures, and became one of the most successful archaeologists the world has ever known. He discovered the hidden entrance to the Great Pyramid and found his way into the central burial chamber; he opened up tombs in the Valley of the Kings and cleared away the sand that had filled up the entrances to lots of ancient temples.

Tons of stuff found by Belzoni and other adventurers were sent back and put on display in European museums, which means that people like you and me can go and see what all the fuss was about without having to travel all the way to Egypt.

So if you're an Egyptomaniac who can't afford the plane ticket, take a trip to a museum and have a look at what they've got!

Grrrr!

EGYPTIANS TIMELINE

3000 BC	Early hieroglyphs are invented
	Upper and Lower Egypt are united, with Memphis as the capital city
2500 BC	The Great Pyramid and the Sphinx are built in Giza
2200 BC	Over in Asia, Chinese civilization begins
1800– 1650 BC	The Hyksos move into the north of Egypt and set up their own kingdom
1525 BC	Egyptians start burying their dead Pharaohs in the Valley of the Kings
around 1480 BC	Egyptians win the Battle of Megiddo, and take home masses of booty
1473– 1458 BC	Hatshepsut the female Pharaoh rules Egypt
1336– 1327 BC	Pharaoh Tutankhamun rules Egypt

525 BC	The Persians invade Egypt under Cambyses II
509 BC	The Romans start a republic in Italy
450 BC	Herodotus the Greek writes his guidebook to Egypt
332 BC	Alexander the Great conquers Egypt
305 BC	The first Ptolemy takes over Egypt
48 BC	Julius Caesar visits Egypt
30 BC	Cleopatra kills herself with a snake; Egypt becomes part of the Roman Empire
27 AD	Jesus begins teaching in Judea, and starts something big
Fourth century AD	The Romans become Christian, and ban hieroglyphs and the Egyptian gods
1799	The Rosetta Stone is discovered
1815	Giovanni Belzoni goes to Egypt to lug heavy stones about
1922	Howard Carter discovers King Tut's tomb

EGYPTIANS QUIZ

1 Which is the only one of the Seven Wonders of the World still standing?

2 What's the coolest colour to paint your Egyptian house?

3 What was a Pharaoh's favourite pet?

4 Why was it odd that Pharaoh Hatshepsut had a beard?

5 Where can you see Cleopatra's Needle?

6 Which god had the head of a falcon?

7 Whose brother chopped him into bits and scattered him all over the desert?

8 What does the Egyptian word 'miew' mean?

9 What can you cure by eating a mouse cooked in oil?

10 Who named 14 different cities after himself?

Also available in this series

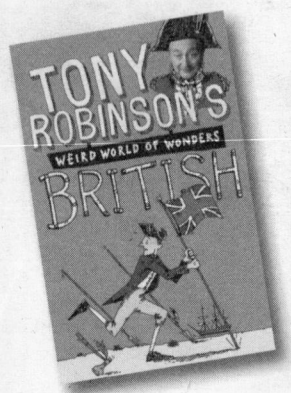

PLAY THE
AWESOME
WEIRD WORLD
OF WONDERS
GAME
NOW AT

www.weirdworldofwonders.com